This book belongs to:

This edition published by Yosif Limited Ltd in 2018

Yosif Limited Ltd
27 Lilburn Crescent
Massey, Auckland 0614
New Zealand
www.yosif.co.nz
admin@yosif.co.nz

Printed by CreateSpace, An Amazon.com Company

Yosif Travel Books – New Zealand

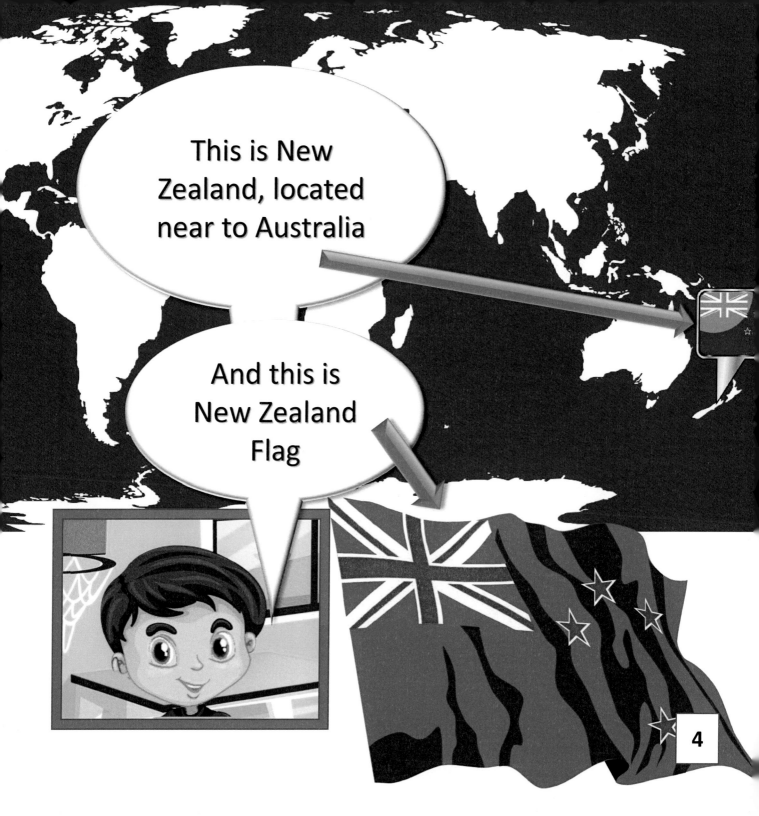

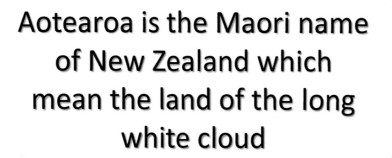

Aotearoa is the Maori name of New Zealand which mean the land of the long white cloud

Wellington is the capital

WELLINGTON

5

New Zealanders are also called Kiwis ..... But kiwi is not a fruit

It is New Zealand native flightless bird

7

New Zealanders is the home to

Yellow-eyed penguin

Kea

30 million sheep

Fur seal

Tui

The kiwi bird

Fantail

The blue penguin

Fiordland crested penguin

8

No matter where you are in New Zealand, you'll never be more than 128 km from the seaside

www.peaceful-design.com

In New Zealand there is a

Giant kiwifruit in
Te Puke

Giant Kiwi bird in
Otorohang

Giant soft drink
bottle in Paeroa

Giant donut in
Springfield

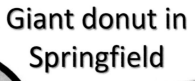

11

Don't miss Kelly Tarlton's Sea Life Aquarium in Auckland for fun underwater discovery

Auckland

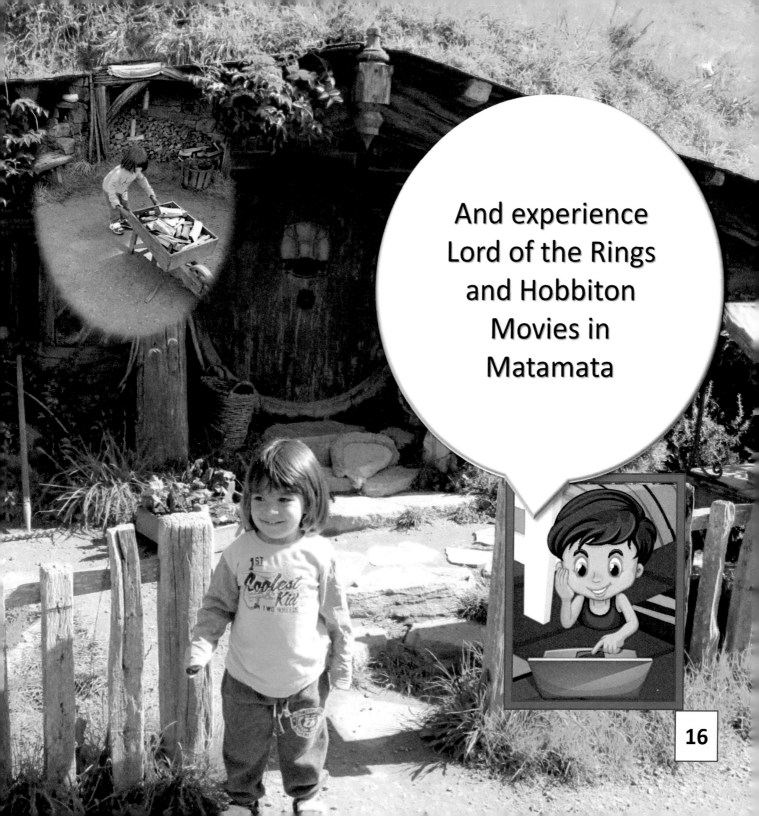

And experience Lord of the Rings and Hobbiton Movies in Matamata

16

Butterfly Creek in Auckland is a place that brings butterflies, dinosaurs, playgrounds and train sets

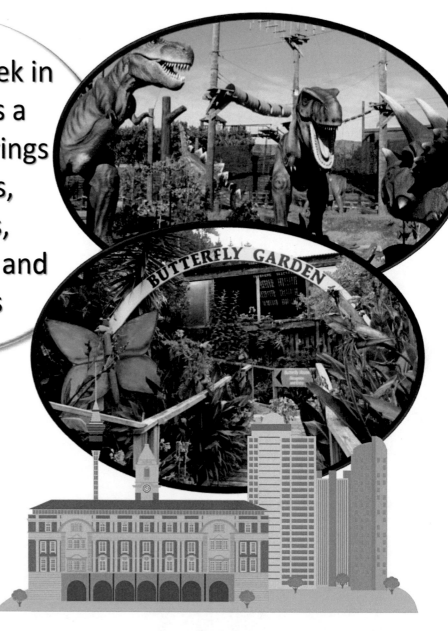

Auckland

Also MOTAT the museum of transport and technology ,,, Amazing

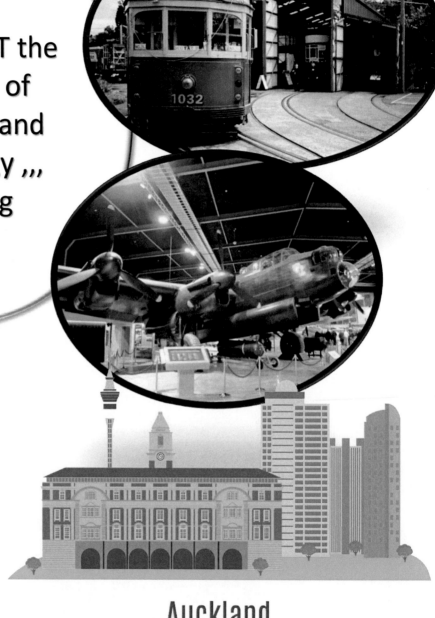

Auckland

If you want to interact with sheep, horses, ducks, goats, piglets you should visit Kiwi Valley Farm Park and Maze in Auckland too

Auckland

In Rotorua, enjoy your magical journey in

3D Trick Art Gallery

Skyline Rotorua Luge and Gondola

Rainbow Springs

Have I told you about Zealandia in Wellington, home to some of New Zealand's most rare wildlife. You should take your mum and dad there

Wellington

For the south island, I visited Christchurch with my dad twice and I really enjoyed

Riding the Tram

Visiting Adrenalin forest

25

Christchurch

Christchurch

26

31

Made in the USA
San Bernardino, CA
11 August 2018